UNEXPECTED
DIALOGUE

Mike Street & Joe O'Neill

FM Fine Art Gallery
Los Angeles, CA

July 2016

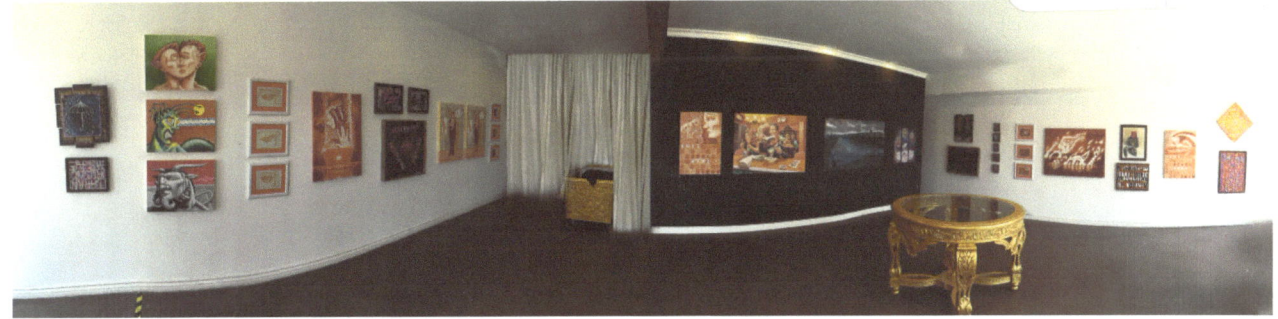

Curated by Karrie Ross

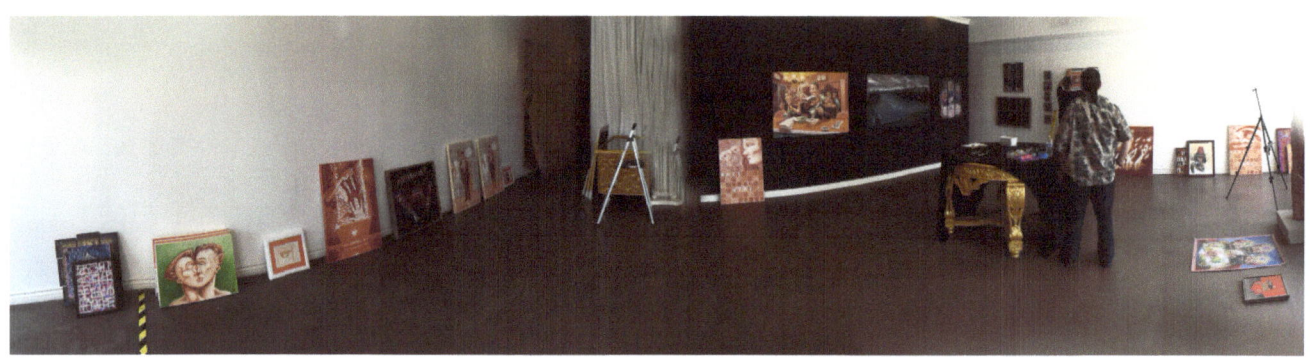

Unexpected Dialogue

with Mike Street & Joe O'Neill
Curated by Karrie Ross

Karrie Ross: 708 W. 140th Street, Gardena, CA 90347
Visit her website at www.KarrieRoss.com.

Printed in the United States of America

Book Design by Karrie Ross

Unexpected Dialogue

lan·guage
/ˈlaNGgwij/

noun

1. the method of human communic
   structured and conventional way
   "a study of the way children lear

2. the system of communication us
   "the book was translated into tw
   synonyms: tongue, mother tong

di·a·logue
/ˈdīəˌläg, ˈdīəˌlôg/

noun

1. conversation between two c
   "the book consisted of a ser
   synonyms: conversation, tal

verb NORTH AMERICAN

1. take part in a conversation c
   "he stated that he wasn't go

con·ver·sa·tion
/ˌkänvərˈsāSH(ə)n/

noun

the informal exchange of ideas by spoken words.
"the two men were deep in conversation"
synonyms: discussion, talk, chat, gossip, tête-à-tête, hear

- an instance of this.
  "she picked up the phone and held a conversation in Fr

We don't communicate without a language of some kind—see, hear, taste, smell, touch, intuit—are all sense *languaging*/vibration. Each artist develops a special-to-them tone—that "thing" that GETS them going. Each artwork created is a note in their vibration. A series of artwork is a continuation of the "tone range" as it binds the art together and the vibration begins to be felt on a more conscious level—*dialogue*. Then BAM! the vibration becomes so strong, so loud, so in-your-face that its a *conversation* that must be acknowledged...and shared.

Mike and Joe's work have a unique language when viewed alone, and a dialogue when viewed together. With images verging on surreality or the subconscious mind, both artists pose questions of challenge creating a lively conversation. A vibration that has nothing to do with if they are similar or how different in style or medium or subject.

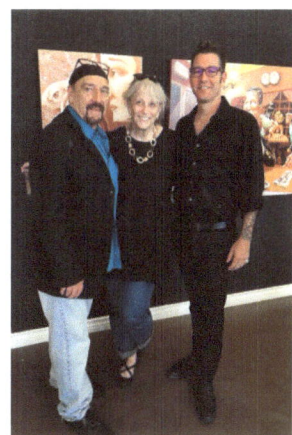

On the following pages please enjoy their artwork and read how each artist reflects on their work within the dynamics of personal language, dialogue, and conversaton.

July 2016

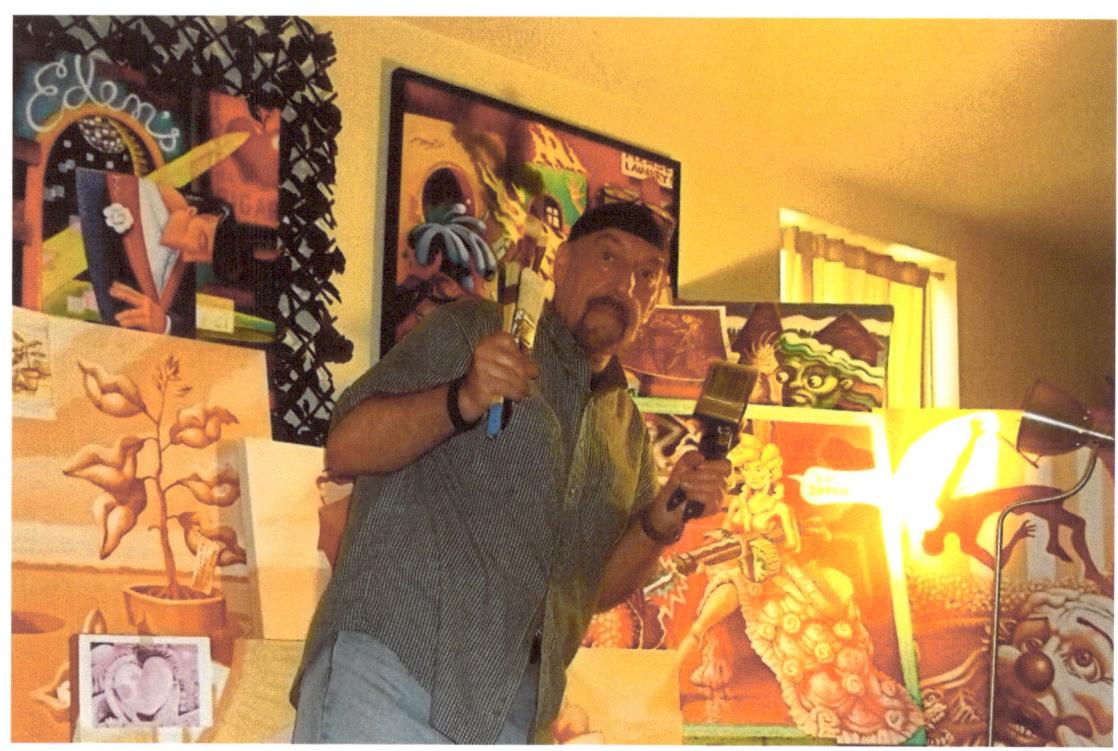

Mike in studio

Mike Street

language : dialogue : conversation

Every artwork has its own language through which it expresses and communicates. My narratives tend to be familiar and ubiquitous situations in some ways, and strange personal dreamworlds in others. Caricatured archetypes romp in simplified but twisted environments of memory, exaggeration, thick paint and stylized shapes. Although I love color, several recent paintings have been rendered in values of brown. Among the many reasons for this, the lack of color seems to evoke an elegant Old World charm while diffusing the cartoonish aspects. Whimsy is darkened, and the unreal becomes more real. In this retroactive language of brown, newness and oddity can easily step forward with impact and acceptance.

I often work in large thematic series to explore and exhaust my varied interests. Within each series, the dialogue among individual pieces begins with the comparison of obvious common denominators (like media, size, presentation, etc.) Of course, the dialogue becomes richer and more interesting when the structured continuity is disrupted by the untamed differences. Each piece contributes in this sublime conflict, revealing and embellishing autobiographical details. The dialogue is a chatterbox's diary disguised as an illustrated storybook.

As my fanciful characters and places collide with reality and common sense, I'm certain the conversation outcome is more than I ever intended. Unlikely juxtapositions and magical mash-ups create riddles to solve and games to play. A lot is left unsaid in the conversation. There is an invitation, maybe a seduction, to safely participate and navigate in even the most "difficult" topics such as death and sexuality. As evidenced by the smaller studies, many of my larger paintings are calculated strategies. Thinking before speaking, I try to ensure that the work is delightful enough to enter – and thoughtful enough to linger.

July 2016

Unexpected Dialogue

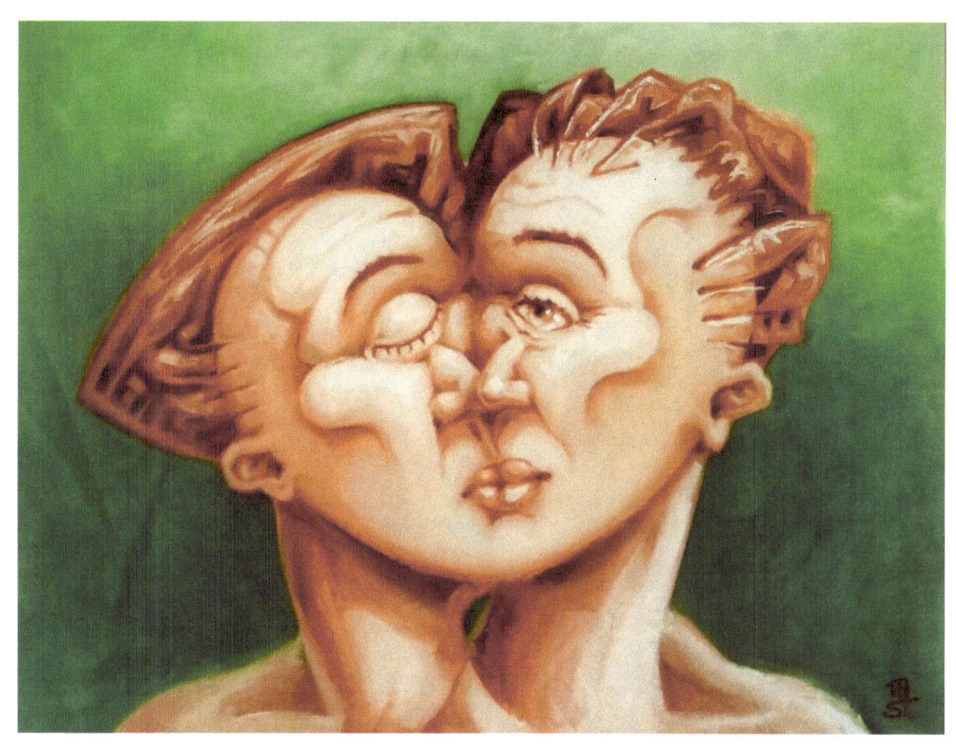

CYCLOPS LOVE
(Mt. Olympus Below the Tree Line Series)
18x24 inches
Oil on canvas mounted on wood panel
2008

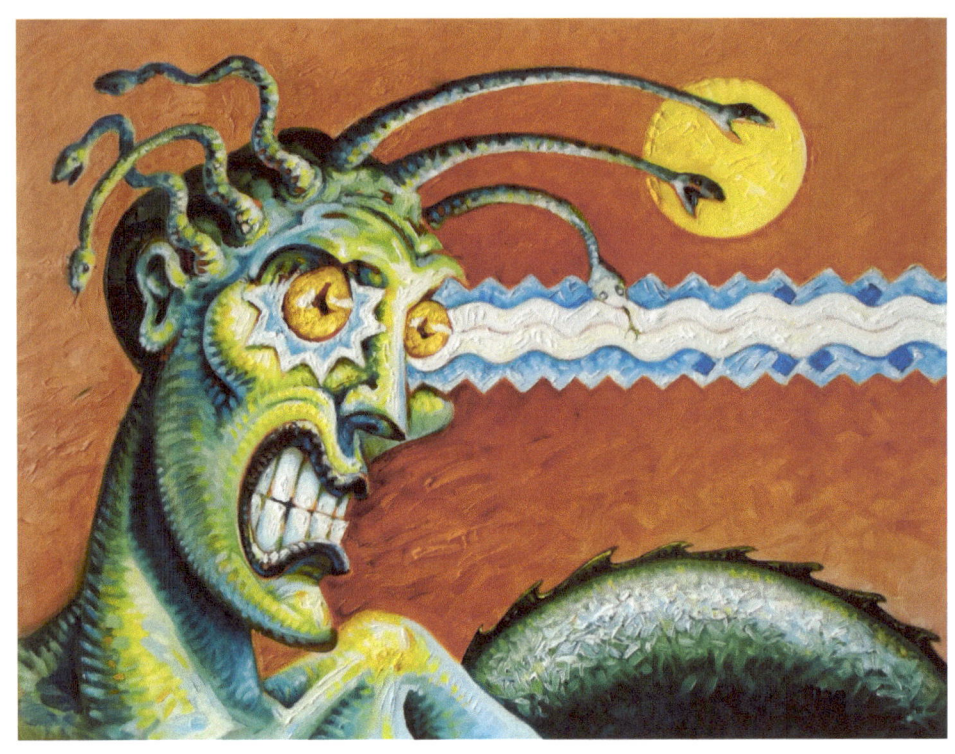

MEDUSA, PISSED OFF
(Mt. Olympus Below the Tree Line Series)
18x24 inches
Oil on canvas mounted on wood panel
2008

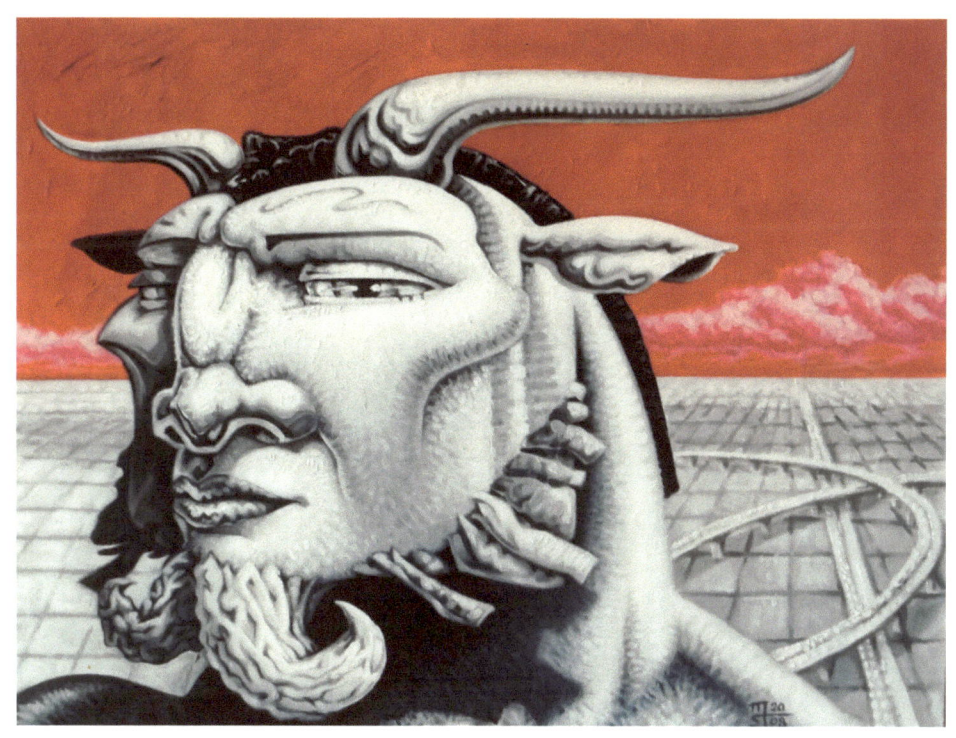

MINOTAUR AND LABYRINTH
(Mt. Olympus Below the Tree Line Series)
18x24 inches
Oil on canvas mounted on wood panel
2008

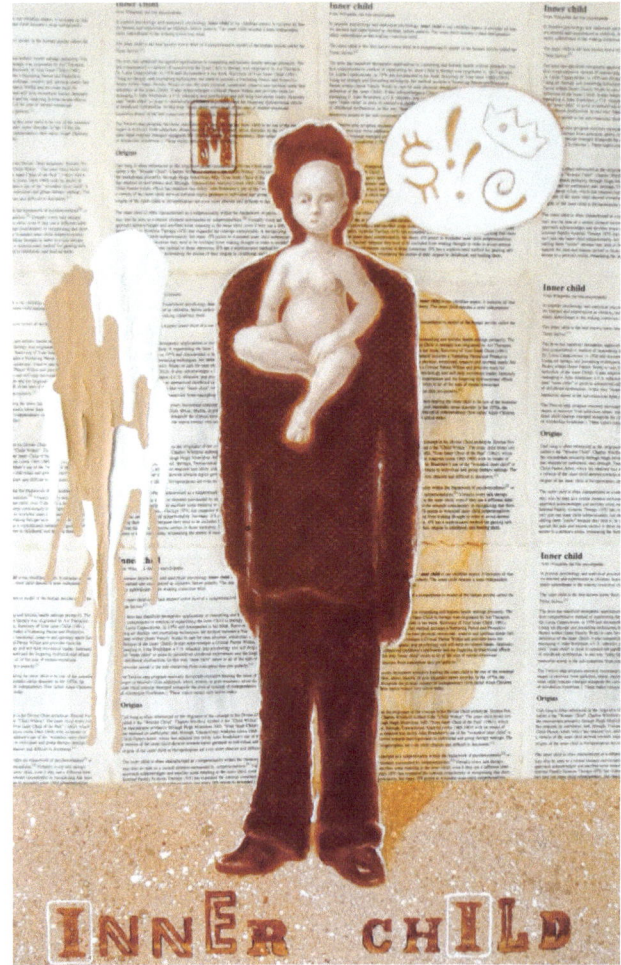

INNER CHILD (MALE)
24x36 inches
Mixed media on stretched canvas
2016

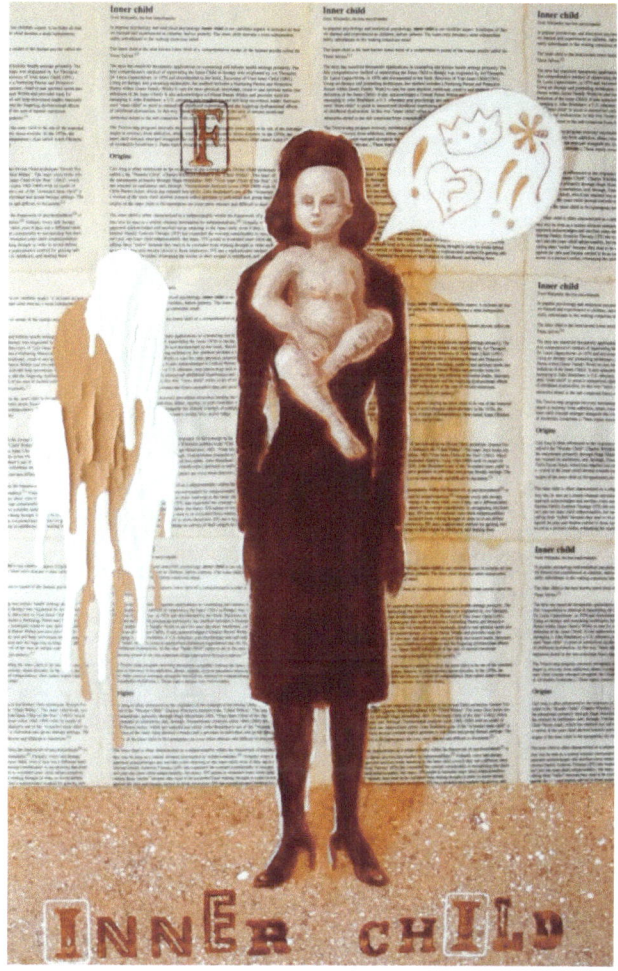

INNER CHILD (FEMALE)
24x36 inches
Mixed media on stretched canvas
2016

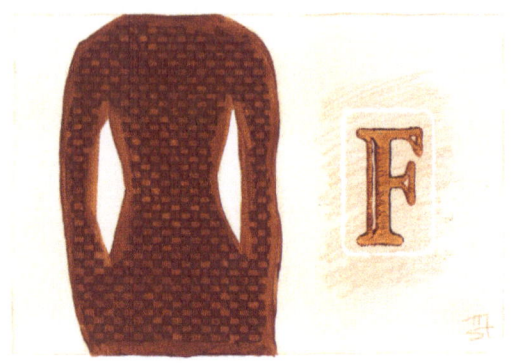

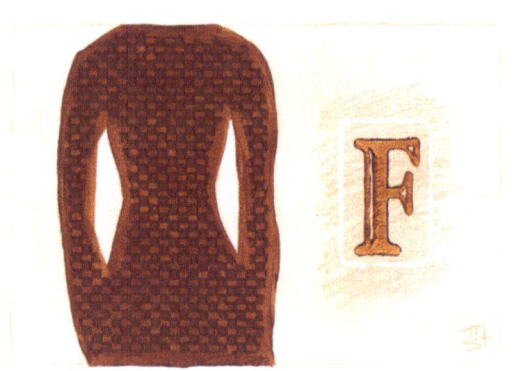

INNER CHILD STUDY (FEMALE)
9x12 inches
Mixed media on canvas
2016

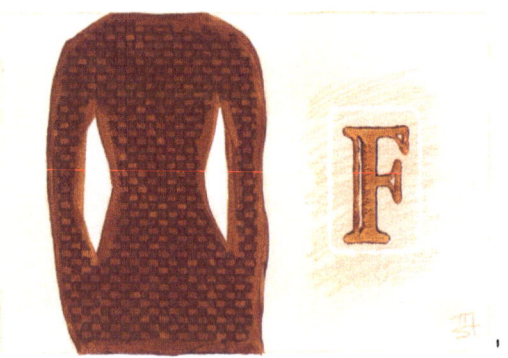

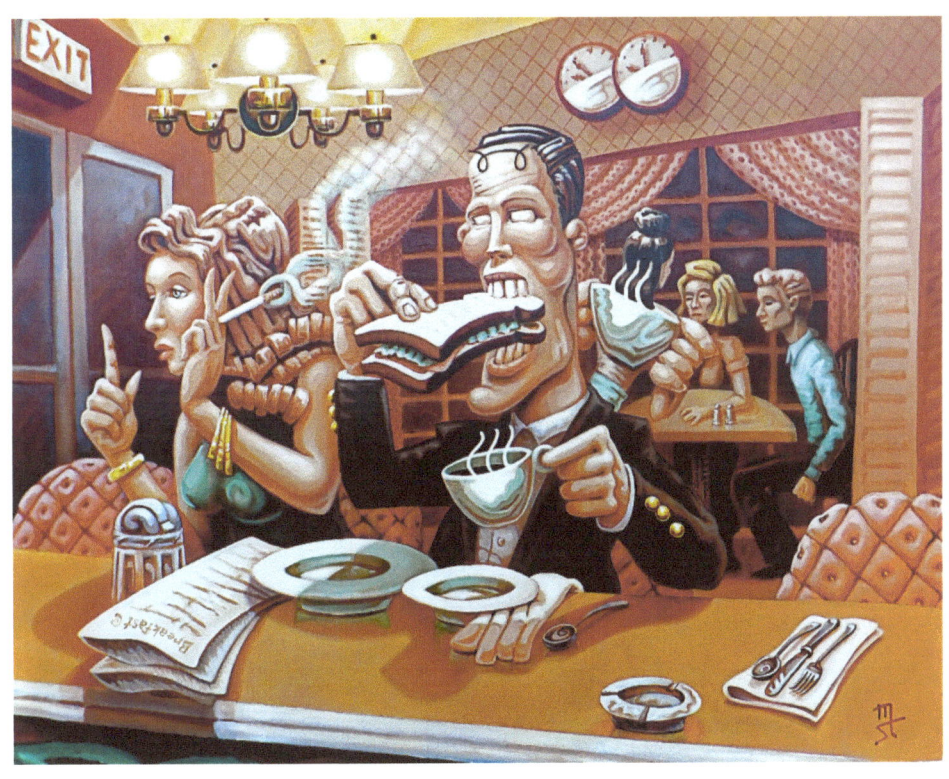

LUNCHING WITH MR. SMEARCASE
36x48 inches
Oil on stretched canvas
2011

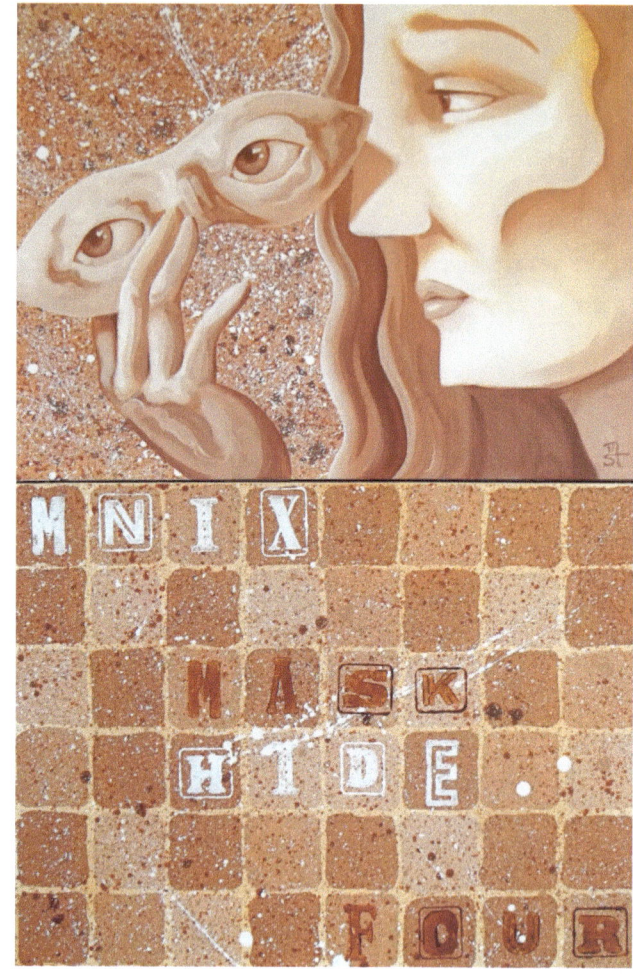

MASK (FOUR Letter Word Series)
24x36 inches, diptych
Mixed media on canvas mounted on wood panels
2016

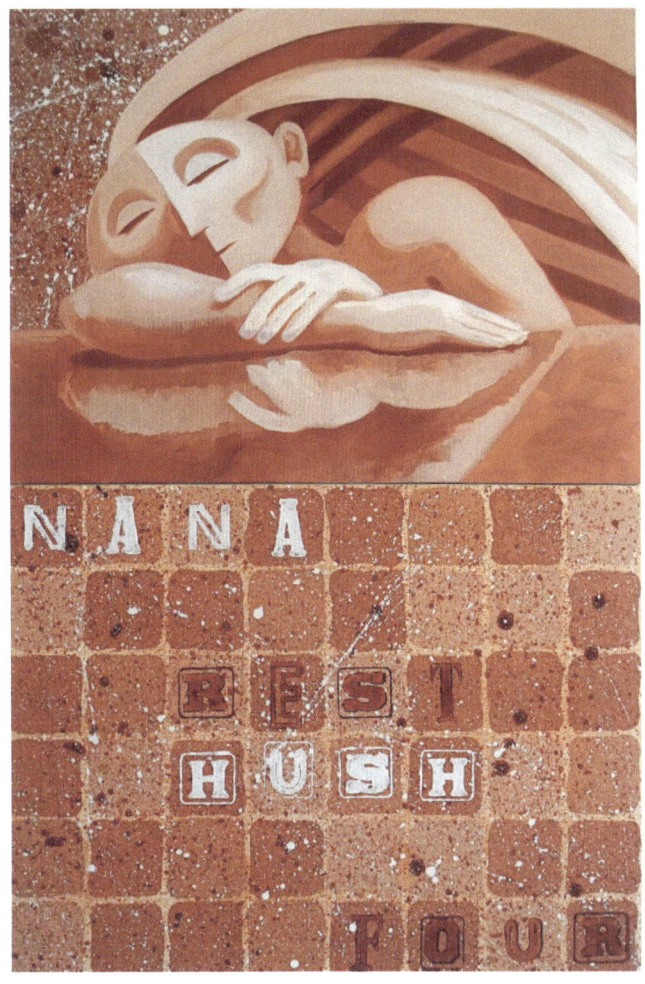

REST (FOUR Letter Word Series)
24x36 inches, diptych
Mixed media on canvas mounted on wood panels
2016

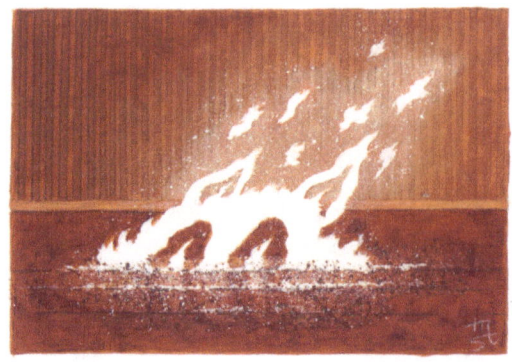

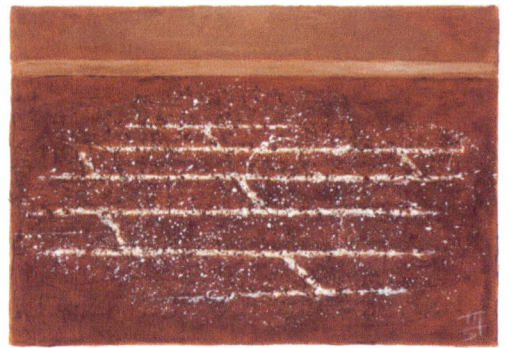

CATS BURNING THE FLOOR
STUDY
9x12 inches
Mixed media on canvas
2016

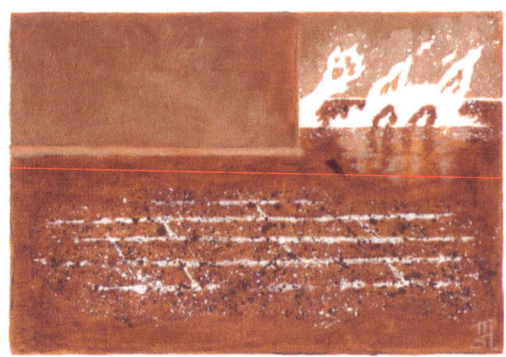

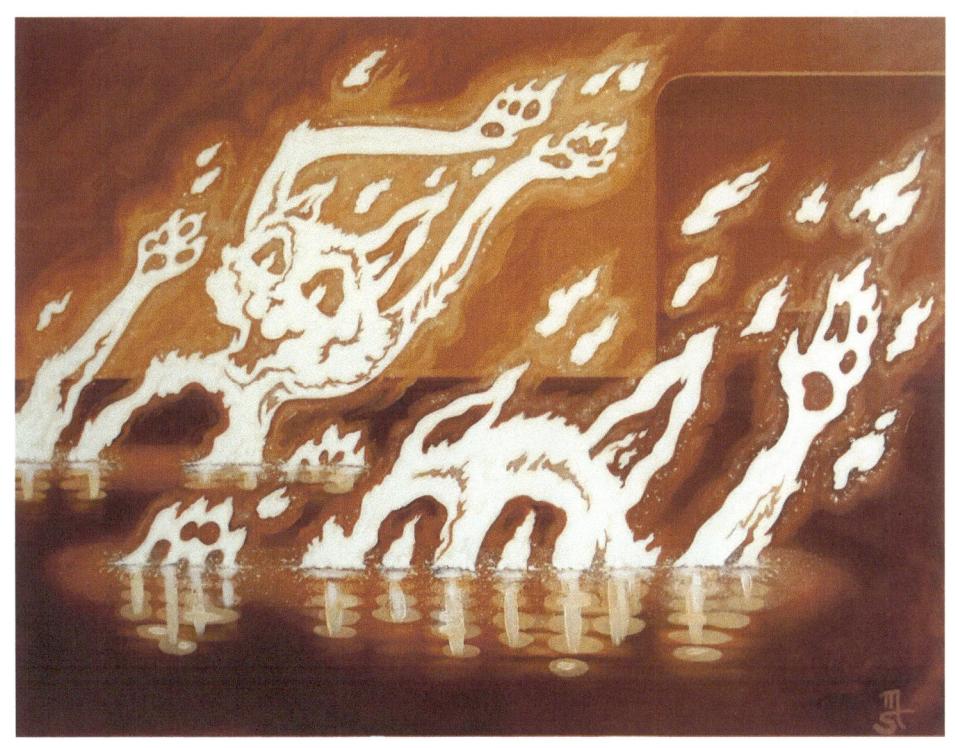

CATS BURNING THE FLOOR
36x48 inches
Mixed media on stretched canvas
2016

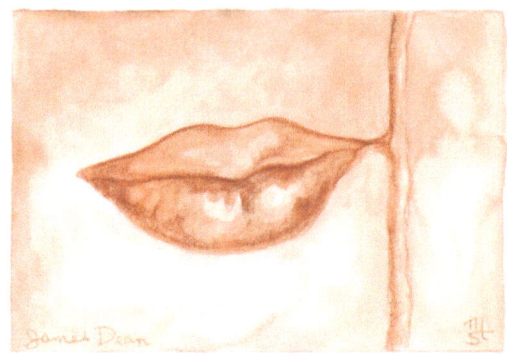

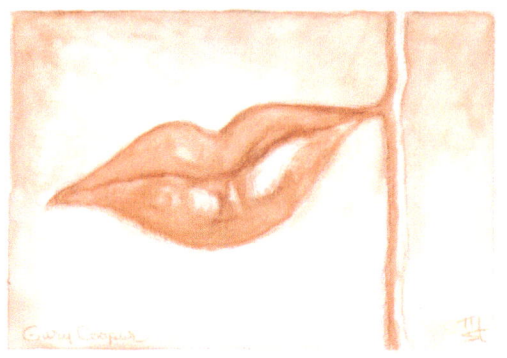

RECYCLING PLANT STUDY
(Gary Cooper, James Dean, James
Stewart)
9x12 inches
Mixed media on canvas
2016

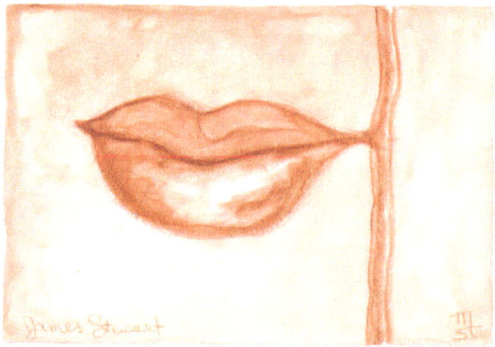

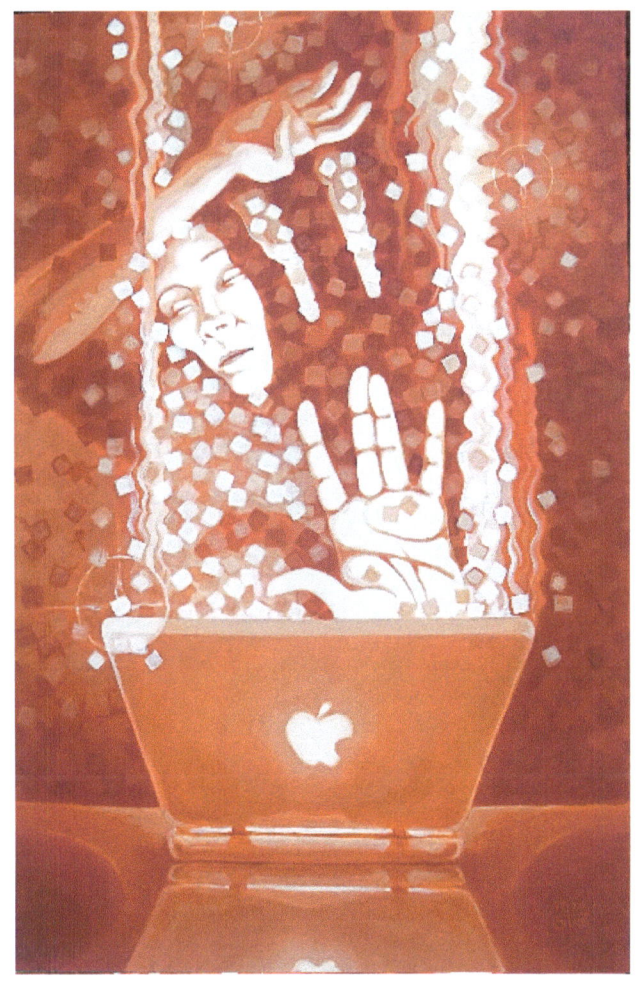

PANDORA'S BOX
24x36 inches
oil on stretched canvas
2016

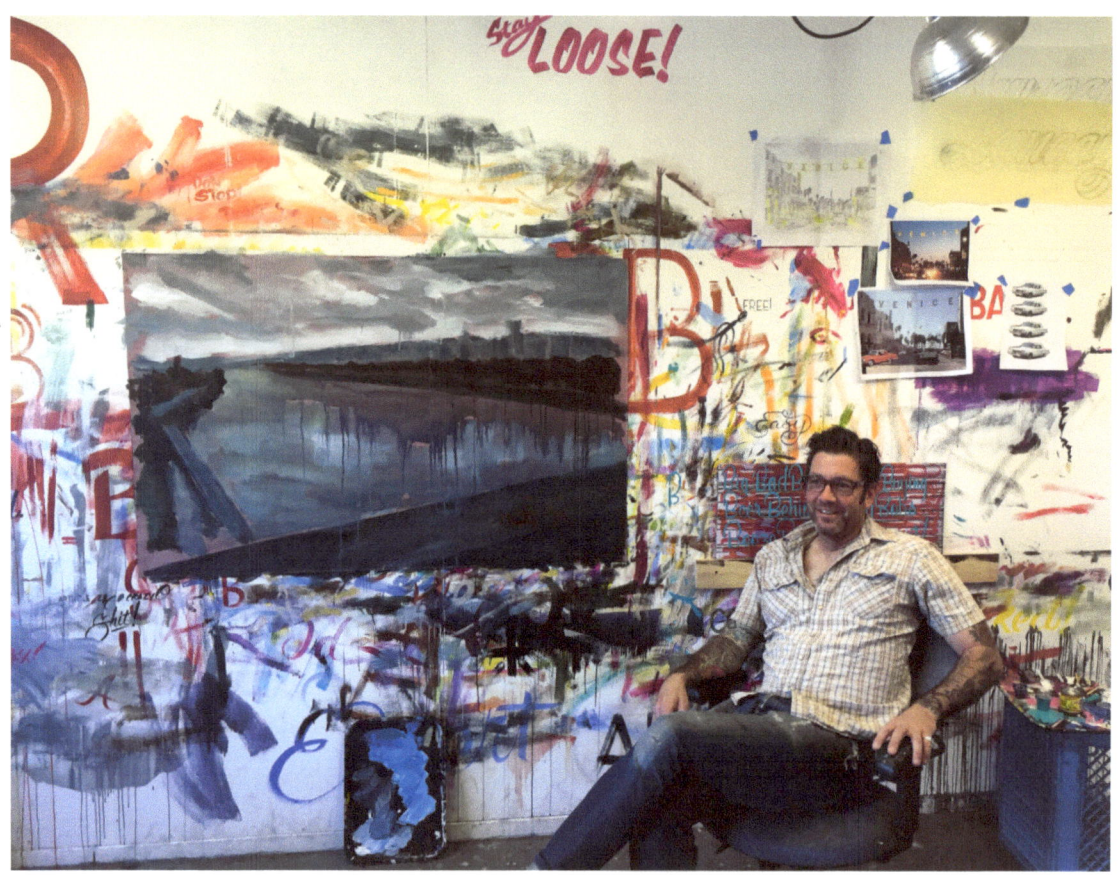

Joe in studio

Joe O'Neill

language : dialogue : conversation

There is a problem with using words in a painting (as I do)- it is too easy for the word's meanings to become the focus of the work. I'm interested in letters (and by extension, words) as another visual element in a painting. They may relate to the images, there may be a specific statement written with the words in the painting but the words are obscured for good reason. Even though the painting maybe about a specific subject or have a specific images in it I want people to have room for their own interpretation, not just be bound to mine. In addition, my experience with the painting once it is finished is essentially as an artifact of an experience, that being the act of making the painting. It is in the past for me, but the viewer experiences it is the present. I can't control how they see or interpret it, which is good because they may see it in a completely different way than I intended. That it can potentially generate different interpretations for different viewers indefinitely is what gives the painting life.

www.doubleojoe.com

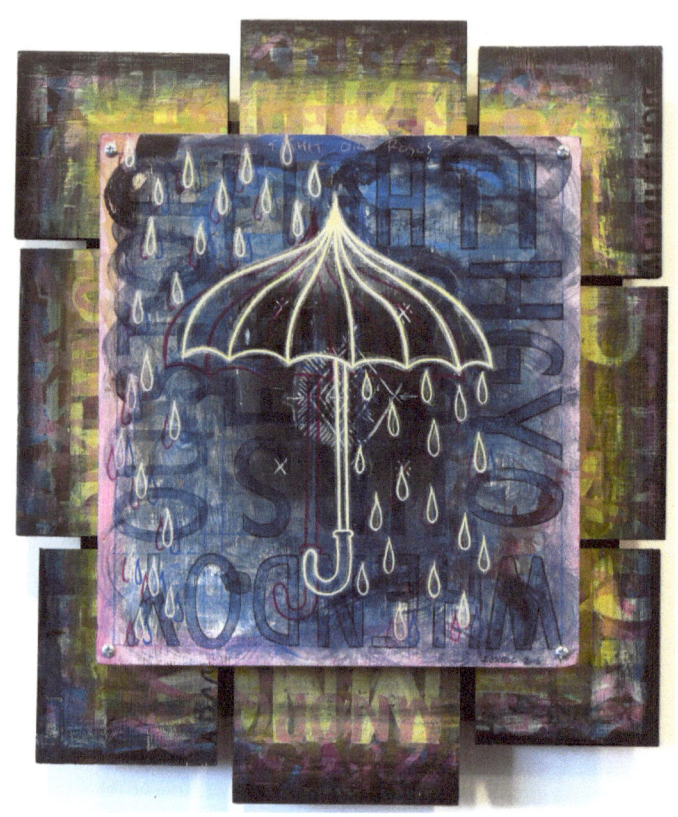

Shit or Roses
acrylic and enamel on wood
18.5 x 21.5
2016

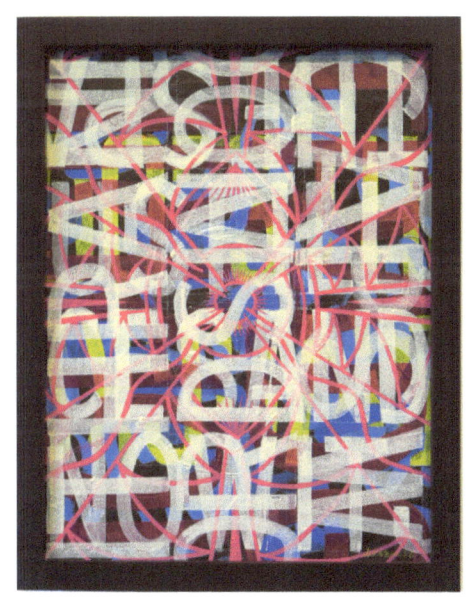

An Actual Conversation (study)
acrylic on canvas
12 x15 framed
2016

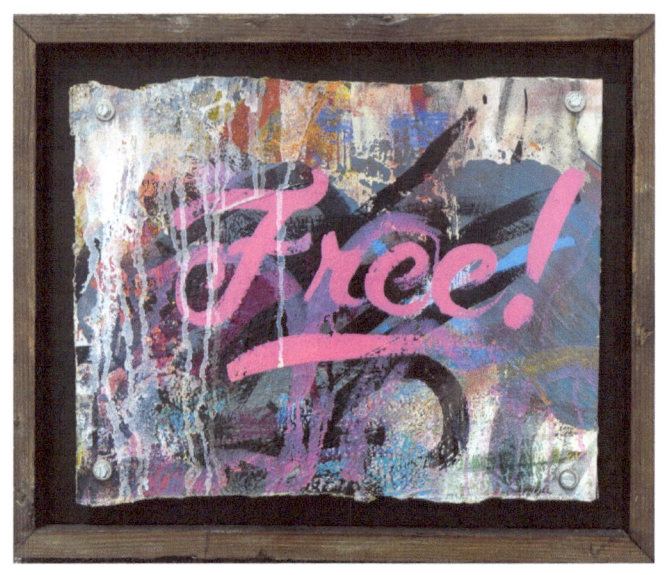

Free
acrylic and enamel on drywall
14 x 17.5 frameed
2013

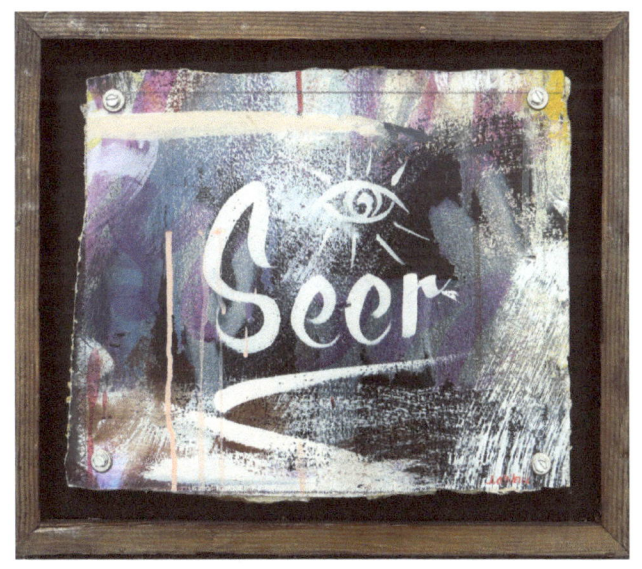

Seer
acrylic and enamel on drywall
13 x 15.5 framed
2013

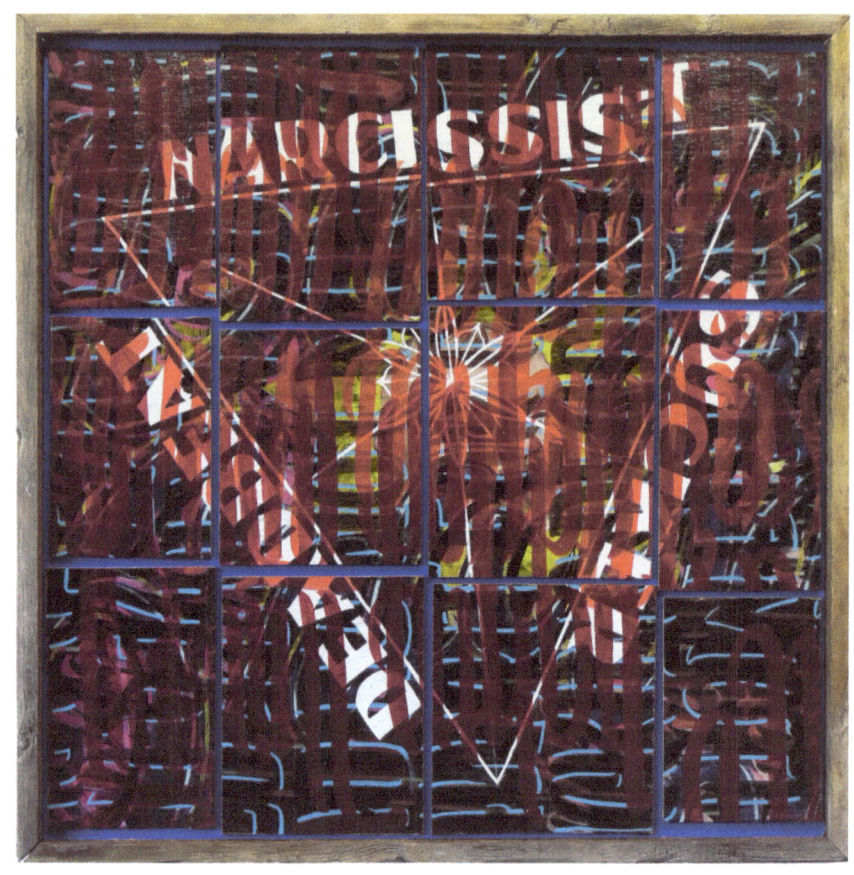

Love Triangle (an old country song)
Enamel on Wood framed
30 x 29.5
2015

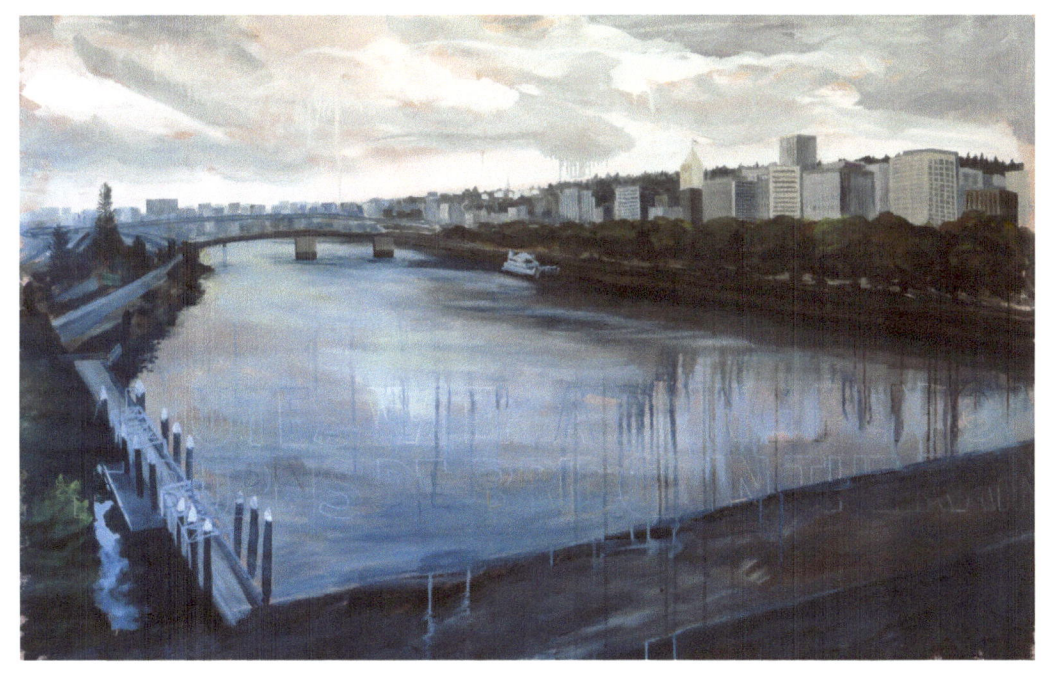

5 Minutes
acrylic on paper
35 x 57
2016

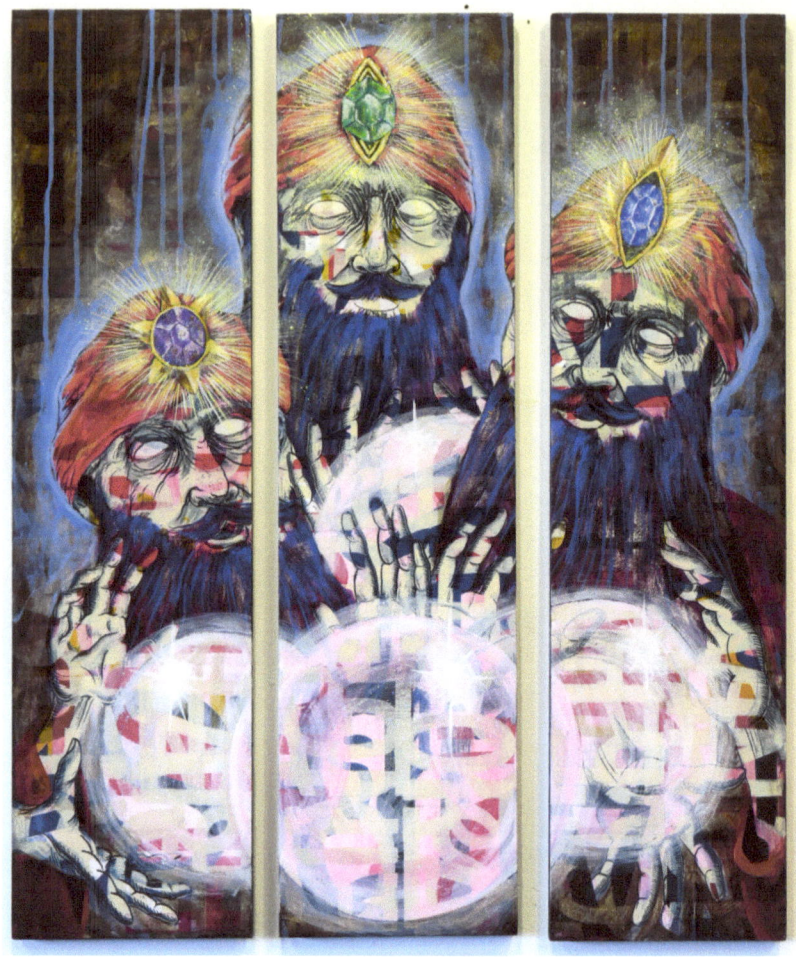

Unexpected Dialogue
acrylic and glitter on wood
triptych- 3 panels
8 x 30 each
2016

Unexpected Dialogue

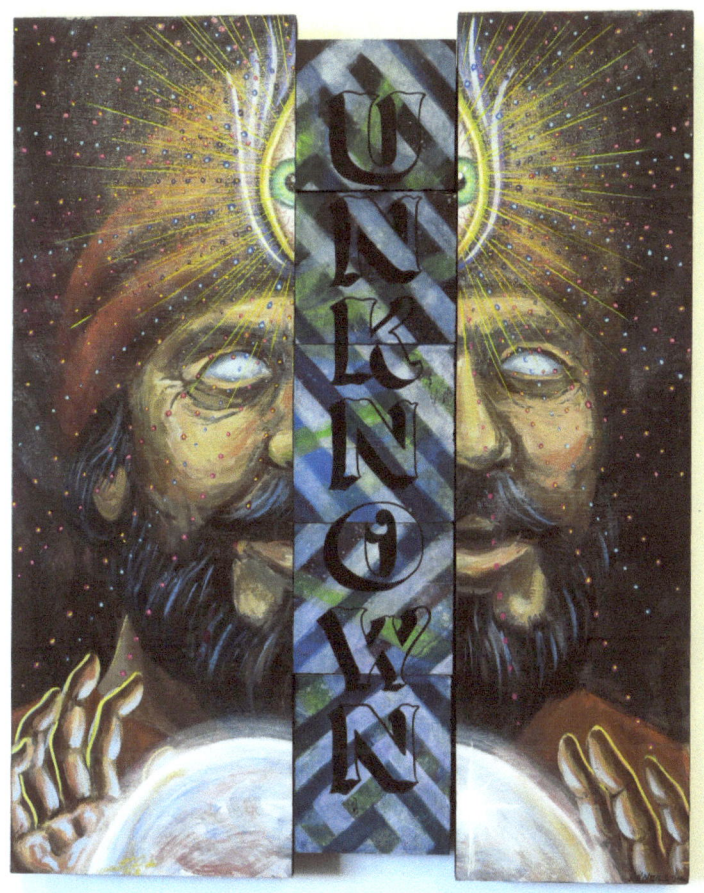

Unknown
acrylic and glitter on wood
19.5 x 24
2016

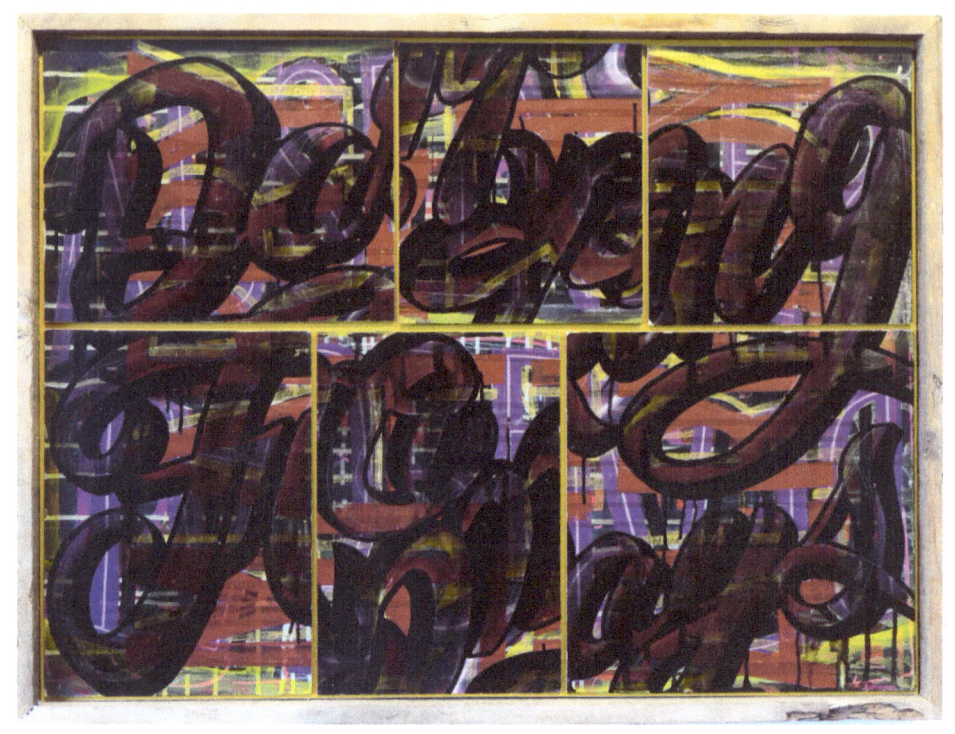

Dark Days
Enamel on Wood
34 x 25 framed
2015

Acrylic and enamel on wood

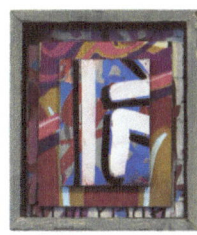

Stack no. 1
6 x 6.75 framed
2016

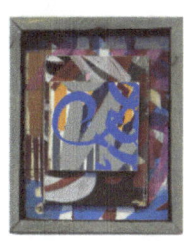

Stack no. 2
5.5 x 6.5 framed
2016

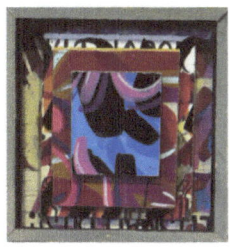

Stack no. 3
6.5 x 6.75 framed
2016

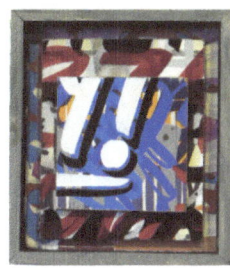

Stack no. 4
6.5 x 7.25 framed
2016

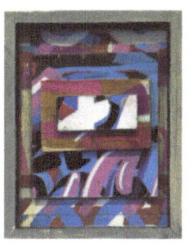

Stack no. 5
5.5 x 6.75 framed
2016

July 2016

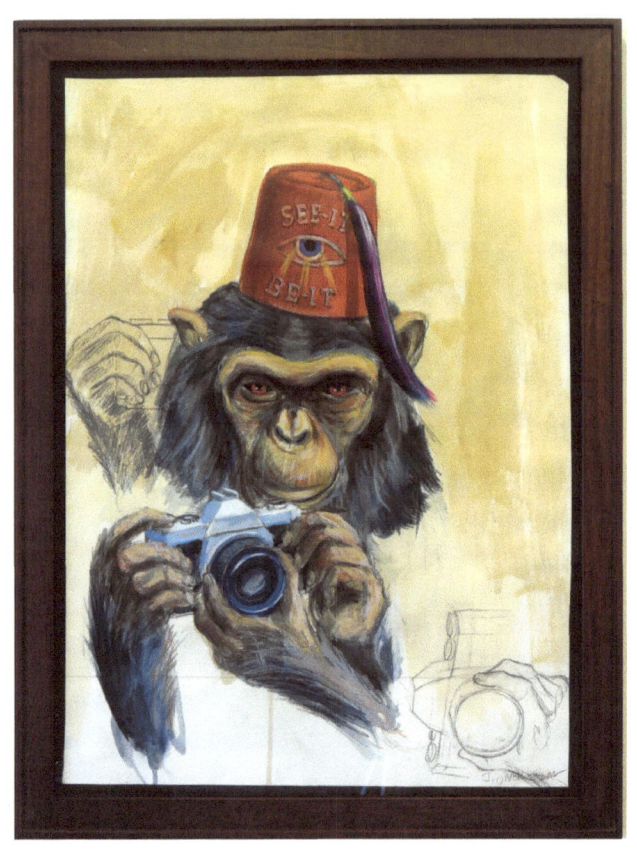

See It Be It (study)
acrylic on paper
20.5 x 26.5 framed
2012

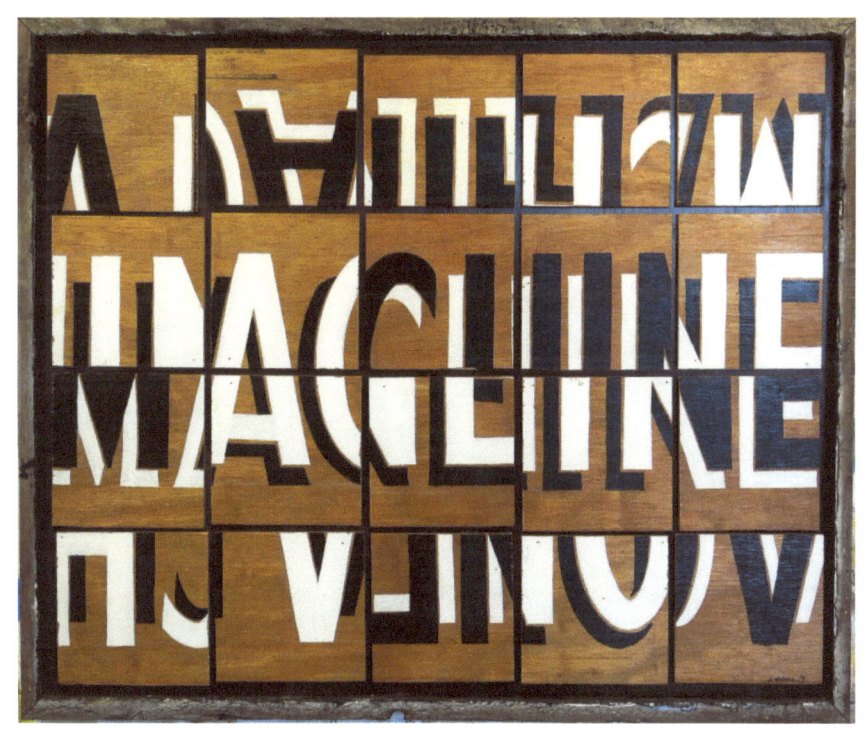

I'm Not a Machine
Enamel on Wood
20.5 x 25 framed
2014

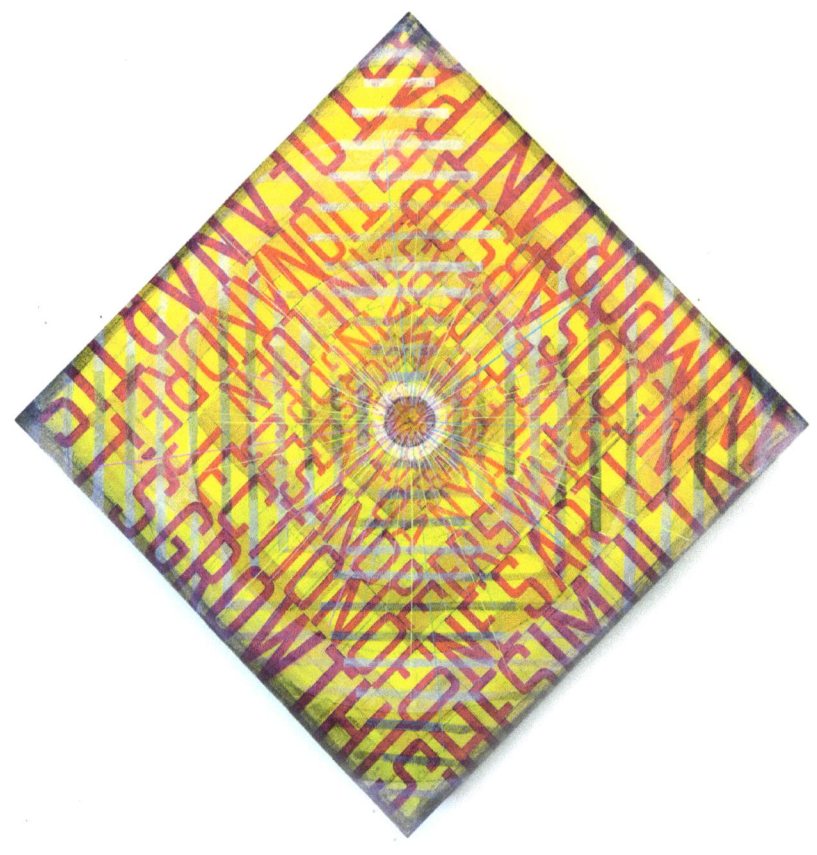

Influence
acrylic on wood
22 x 22
2016

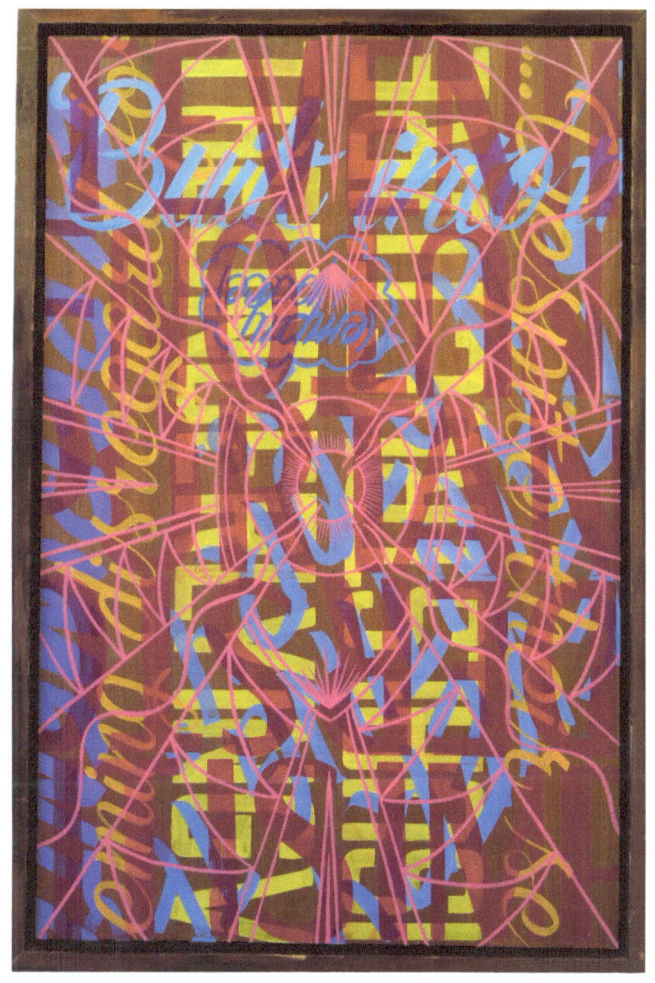

An Actual Conversation
acrylic on wood
22.5 x 33 framed
2016

Mike Street & Joe O'Neil

July 2016. FM Fine Art Gallery

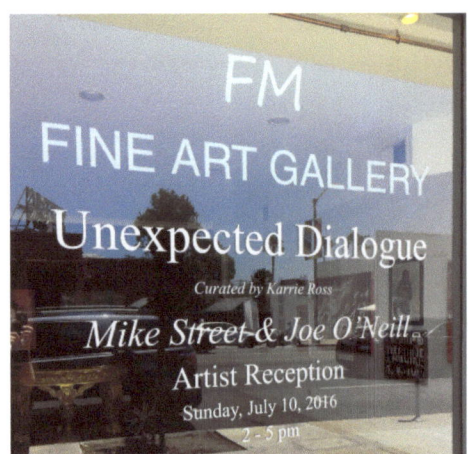

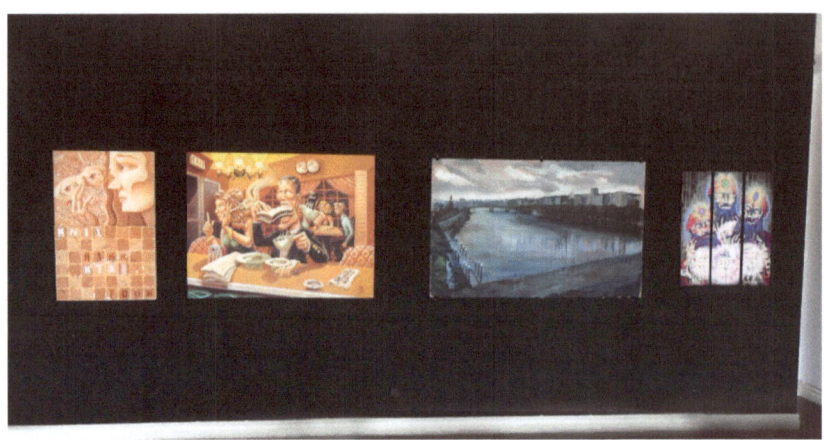

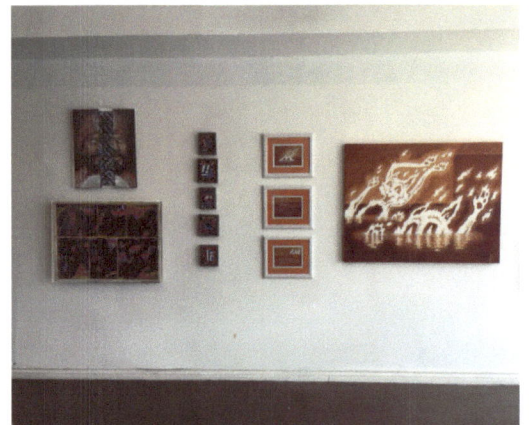

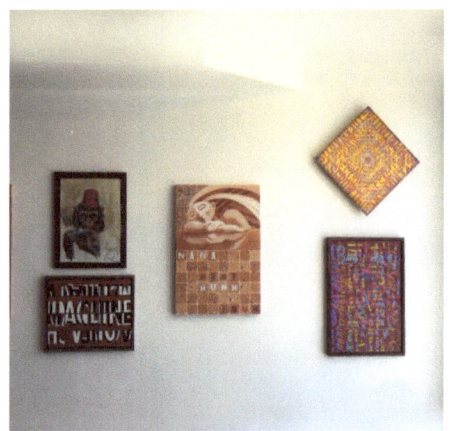

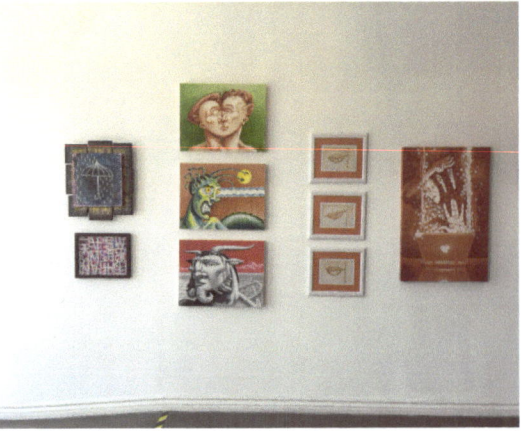

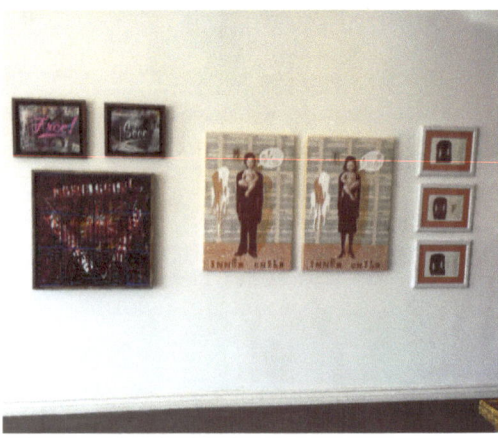

Unexpected Dialogue